Robert Creighton Wright

Echoes from the Blarney stone and other rhymes

Robert Creighton Wright

Echoes from the Blarney stone and other rhymes

ISBN/EAN: 9783337118808

Printed in Europe, USA, Canada, Australia, Japan

Cover: Foto ©Thomas Meinert / pixelio.de

More available books at **www.hansebooks.com**

ECHOES

FROM THE

BLARNEY STONE

AND

OTHER RHYMES

BY

W. C. R.

CHICAGO
CHARLES H. KERR & COMPANY
175 DEARBORN STREET
1889

CONTENTS.

The Blarney Stone	5
"Swaat Rachel," Says I	10
Pat's Disappointment	22
Tim O'Grady	26
The Gintleman That Pays The Rint	38
The Gintleman That Takes The Rint	41
Mary Malue	44
Railroad Mike	47
Pat's Views of a Mother-in-Law	51
Love's Antics	53
How Can Poet Tune The Lyre?	56
A Farewell to Jennie	60
Picnic Dinner Song	62
Duke John	64
Irene	65
Death of an Old Bachelor	66
Four Fair Maids	74
A Valentine	76
A Horse is a Horse	78
Welcome to Spring	80
Smoker Jim	83
A Boy's Wishes	88
A Mother's Care	91
June	93
Tears and Fears	97
Day-break	100
A School-girl's Greeting to Autumn Flowers	106
The Snow Storm	112
Why Should Autumn Bid Adieu?	114

THE BLARNEY STONE.

At Blarney Castle, in the County of Cork, Ireland, is a celebrated stone called the Blarney Stone. It is made famous by the tradition among Irish people that whoever kisses the Blarney Stone will from that moment become gifted with the power of winsome flattery and persuasive eloquence. Hence it is the reputed shrine of ambitious orators and ardent lovers from time immemorial to the present day.

IT'S quare how some can talk so glib,
   And tell what they are seekin'.
They have a knack, and cut of gib,
   And illoquence for speakin',
And they can string so long a chat
   Ye'd wonder how they prate it.
They take a word of this and that,
   And thin, how well they mate it.
And gaping crowds they can entrance
   And lead them on to mobbin',
Or like a fiddle in a dance
   Just kape thim gintly bobbin';
And they can spake the words of pace
   Our doubts and fears dispellin',
Or they can bid our ills inkrease
   Beyond the power of tellin'.
But what's the grass they graze upon
   That kapes their tongues so thriven?
And how is it they saze upon
   Their words woot little striven?

The Blarney Stone, the Blarney Stone,
It has a magic all its own,
And though some fools may mock and hiss it,
The wisest men will stoop to kiss it.

And some there are, O pity, weep!
   Who don't know how to gabble,
Like rocking babes that cannot creep
   They only mouth and babble.
And those there are who can't ixpress
   The igeas that elate them,
It makes them labor to ixcess
   In ordther to rapate them.
And some there are who luve to plase
   And laugh and chat and flatther,
But they have got a dumb dasase,
   And don't know what's the matther.
And oh, the plight of beau or belle,
   Who, thinkin' too intinsely,
Is captured by a quiet spell
   And silence settles dinsely.
For how can they enjoy the hour
   And blessin's that betide them,
When it is not wootin their power
   To chat to one beside them?

The Blarney Stone, etc.

Some Irishmen so oft complain,
   Ye'd think it constant croakin',
But underneath there runs a vein
   That's full of fun and jokin'.
And when young Cupid, up to thricks,
   Has thought just how to plan it,
He puts his project into fix,
   Woot Irishmen to man it.
And ould Columbus niver found,
   Woot all his wide explorin',
A race, in all the world around,
   So dexterous at adorin'.
So apt they are to speak woot grace
   Their igeas of affection,
Their words will find a wilcome place,
   Wootout a close inspection.
And who can tell the reason why
   Their chat is all so winnin',
That when an hour passes by,
   Ye'd think them just beginnin'?

The Blarney Stone, etc.

Ould Erin has a fame of late
   For shamrock and shillaly,
For orators and statesmen great,
   And odther things as raelly.

And there it is that life is gay
   Woot plisures most refinin';
A little fracas ivery day,
   Kapes business from daclinin'.
And when the English ask for rint,
   It's then ye hear a hummin';
Ye know that nothin' can prevint
   The foinest spourt from comin'.
But Erin's sons as gallants are
   The bravest and the rarest,
And thin her daughters are be far
   The choicest and the fairest.
And whin they meet, oh joy komplate!
   Fwhat wit and songs so jolly—
Whince came their compliments so nate,
   That kills ould melancholy?

The Blarney Stone, etc.

The Yankees niver have a wake,
   Or ony rare injoyment,
They think a joke a sad mistake,
   And vory quare imployment.
Just see the creatures, poor as crows!
   No ghost was iver thinner—
Too limited their dandy clothes,
   To hold a healthy dinner.

But Irishmen are full of mirth,
   Good health and hearts intrepid.
The broth of all the bist of earth,
   Too strong to grow insiped.
And in the field of war or luve,
   No matther where ye mate them,
Ye'll find no cooin' turtle dove—
   Its vory hard to bate them.
But how is it they have such wit?
   Came it by eddecation,
Did nature make a gift of it,
   Or was it vaccination?

The Blarney Stone, the Blarney Stone,
It has a magic all its own,
And though some fools may mock and hiss it,
The wisest men will stoop to kiss it.

SWAAT RACHEL, SAYS I.

A MAN that's in business may sometimes delay
To lay down his work and go home to his teay.
For often it's neeadful to stop in the store
And finish the trade that was stharted before,
To count up the cash and lay goods on the shilf,
To fould up his smiles and raturn to himsilf,
To answer some letthers or chat woot a frind,
Till time is ixpended he did not intind.
Woot a glance at his watch he behoulds his mistake,
And thin for his hat and his home he will brake.
His steps are so nimble they hasten his speed,
And nothin' will stop him, no nothin', indeed.
The pigs and the childer, fwhativer may stray
In the front of his path should abandon the way,

And chickens and donkeys and all in the strate,
Know business is business and bate a ratrate.
He cuts across corners, down alleys he glides,
He sails like a ship that is swept by the tides;
Fwhat signifies finces and hedges that lay
In the course of a man that is late for his teay?
His walk may be reckless, but fwhat does he care—
It's home that he's bint and it's time that he's thare.
Now fwhat is the magnet that draws him so quick,
Is it hunger or luve or the fear of a stick?
There's impulse in hunger, there's power in luve,
There's sthringth in ould barley to make a man rove ;
But bist of inventions there's nothin' to bate
The wife of a man when at tea he is late.

It happened just lately that Timothy Hone
Dropped into the store fwhen I was alone.
"Now, Pathrick," says he, "why idle and pine;

Let's be gone to McGaffey's and sample his wine.
We'll neighbor woot Plisure, that's livin' so near,
We'll pay our raspicts and diwide the good cheer;
We'll joke and we'll gossip and gather good news,
Till we drive away care and demolish the blues;
We'll excavate spourt and we'll liberate joy,
And we'll fome on the top of the fun there, me boy.
We'll ordther the bist from the top of the shilf—
So come along, Pathrick, and be there yoursilf."
It's little persuadin' that's iver required,
When somethin's presinted yourself has desired.
The words that he spoke were as yeast in the dough;
They fermented me will and I says that I'll go,
So we sailed like the cars on a Satherday night,

And soon we attinded the shrine of delight.
The curtain may fall on the spourt that we had,
For Rachel might hear it and thin she'd be mad.
We joyed and rajoiced till I thought of me dear,
Then me heart gave a bound as though struck by a spear,
For I knew that me supper was lyin' in state,
And me Rachel was raging at that very date.
So I summoned meself to arise and be gone,
For I knew it was sason that somethin' was done.
The thoughts of me Rachel, they deluged me mind;
They drowned all the spourt I was lavin' behind.
Fwhat could I say to her, how should I dilate
To edify Rachel, me own gintle mate?
I thought and rathought of the thing I chould say,
And the reason that kept me so late for me tay.

I knew she was tinder and kind to the poor,
So I rahashed remarks that had soothed her before.
Said I, " Dearest Rachel, it's late that I am,
But if ye'll be gintle, complasent and calm,
I'll give ye the rason, its all of it true,
I was not at supper, swaat Rachel, woot you.
When down the first street in good sason I came,
I met a poor crature so ragged and lame,
So racked and so haggard woot marks of her woe,
That the cause of her anguish I axed her to know.
She tould me her wee ones were home wootout bread,
Nine childer still livin' and tin of them dead.
I think she's a widdee, bekase she tould me,
Her husband was drownthed in the beautiful sea.
Discoursing still forther she axed me to view
Her goat that was sick; so fwhat could I do?
I journeyed and walked like a man that's humane,
Tin squares up the street and two miles down the lane.

Arrivin' at last at her neat cabin door,
I saw woot me sight fwhat she tould me before.
I helped woot me hand and I wept woot a sigh,
And that's fwhat delayed me, swaat Rachel," says I.
But Rachel's eye flashed and she rose like a queen.
"So, Pathrick, it's courtin' the widdes ye's been!
Enough of you, Pathrick, it's this vory night
I'll pack up me things and be out of your sight."
I knew by her talk and the way that she frowned,
I'd bether fall back and surrinder some ground.
So I fished up a smile on me face and I spoke:
"It's funny, swaat Rachel, ye can't take a joke;
Whin jokes are uncommon I thought ye'd enjoy,
This one I made up woot the use of alloy.
I've seen narry widdee; ye know they are rare,

So banish all fears and dismiss your despair.
When passin' the church they inwited me in,
And I walked to the seat where we always have been.
But missin' me Rachel I thought not to stay
But a vory short time till I'd go on me way.
But the pracher prached grandly and axed us to give
Support to poor cratures that hardly can live.
And said that, whin inded the sermon, they'd take
A colliction from all for just charity's sake.
Now how could I rise and retrate from me pew,
For peaple would say, 'He's a stingy ould screw.'
So I sat and I sat till I thought I would die,
And that's fwhat delayed me, swaat Rachel," says I.
But the sceptical grin that appeared on her face,
Conwinced me me statement was quite out of place.
"You story," said she, "for I sat in the pew,

And I saw not the sign nor the symbol of
    you ;
Contrive woot more skill or I'll pound yer
    ould pate,
Till ye give me good rason for fwhy you are
    late."
"Now, Rachel, be patient, this last that I
    said,
Was sintiment uttered when out of me head.
Our docther waylaid me and dosed me so
    strong–
I lay on the counther for two hours long;
A sick man I am, and hince I reply,
That's just fwhat delayed me, swaat Rachel,"
    says I.
"Now, Pathrick, it sthrikes me," she gal-
    lantly said,
"Ye are nearer the truth fwhen ye'r out of
    your head.
This last of ye'r rasons I cannot despise,
'Twould make any one sick to have in thim
    such lies."
"Trush, trush, now, me Rachel, I'm sorry
    to see
Opinions dewiden me darlin' and me.
Just wait till I've tindered me line of
    excuse,

Before ye cramate me woot cruel abuse.
There's one of yer neighbors that's greatly to blame,
And if ye demand it, I'll give ye his name.
Bod luck to Tim Grady, the crooked ould stick,
Of fraud and deciption he's full as a tick.
The night was quite darruk, and he led the way,
And fwhat do you think, but he steered me astray.
Right east I had started when he says it's west;
And he says I know that this way is the best.
And he says to follow; but I did reflect
To think of the course that was clearly direct.
But finally, politeness caused me to comply,
And that's fwhat delayed me, swaat Rachel," says I.
"Now, Pathrick," says she, "ye are talkin' too blind,
I know there's a rason that lingers behind;
It's drinkin' ye's been, ye scurvy-plagued crone,
I'll fly to me folks, and I'll lave ye alone,"

"Now, Rachel, still listen, I've tased ye so
    long,
Me conscience condimns me for treatin' ye
    wrong.
Its time for the facts, and its facts I avow,
That make up the rason I'll give to ye now.
Your birthday soon comin', I thought I
    would get
A jewel to match the bright eyes of me pet.
So I stopped in the stores woot intintions to
    buy,
And that's fwhat delayed me, sweet Rachel,"
    says I.
"Now, Pathrick," says she, "I think and I feel
That in fwhat you've just said there is some-
    thin' ginteel.
For a man to trate kindly the wife that he
    wed,
Ewinces the fact that himself is well-bred.
And could I be certain that arnest ye be,
I'd thruly forgive ye, though late for your
    tea;
So varied your stories, I can not see how
To come at the truth that ye nibble at now."
"Just listen," says I, "If the facts ye
    retain,
Ye'll see at a glance how well I explain.

It may be I varied in fwhat I tould you,
But sure I took nothin' from that which was true.
On one little statement I dare not rely,
So I *multiplied* rasons, swaat Rachel," says I.

And thus we continyed to talk and beguile,
Till the frowns on her face were subdued woot a smile,
And thin our conversin' took vory wide range
Over subjects familiar, and odther ones strange.
And I blessed me good luck and I flatthered me fate,
To think that I won in the racent debate.
Now if ony one wishes the sacret to know,
How I quelled the rabillion that round me did grow,
For the good of mankind I shall not rasarve
The method that helped me the pace to prasarve.
In the midst of commotion that round me did roar,
I masthered me timper as niver before;
I stood like a pilot all calm at the wheel,

And I said ounly that which was stricthly ginteel.
And for an excuse I did crawl and I crept
Till I got to a nate one that she would accept.
And all odther rasons I let them go by
And we settled on that one, me Rachel and I.

PAT'S DISAPPOINTMENT.

ME heart's broken,
   Me soul's broken,
Kase she gave me no token
   O' ginuine luve.
But to her praise be it spoken!
(And sure I'm not jokin')
Though she gave me no token
   O' ginuine luve,
Yet the schmiles on her face,
That did aften take place,
At times so uncommon,
   And saisons so queer,
Frish courage imparted
And made me light-hearted,
Bright Bridget, swaat Bridget!
   Oh, Bridget, me dear.

So railly I thought, sir,
I was not forgot, sir,
And a meetin' why not, sir,
   Could baith of us have?
Whin woot luve's lamps well lighted,
All things could be righted
And we just united,
   In swaat bonds of luve.

But how to achave it
(And sure ye'l belave it)
A puzzle so hard to explain,
That I will not vinture it here.
But hope held me heart up,
And thin I walked part up
To Bridget, swaat Bridget!
   Bright Bridget, me dear.

But words growing aich less,
I soon became spachless,
And Cupid could tache less
   Than iver before.
So I stood there all waiten',
The same thoughts vibratin',
Till me heart began batin'
   Me back to the doour.
Thin I plucked up again, sir,
And vintured back in, sir,
My mission once more to unfold,
   Whin no one but Bridget was near.
Thin I began swately,
And the words they came nately,
Bright Bridget, swaat Bridget!
   Oh, Bridget, me dear.

And ye'er luve, Bridget Hailey,
Devours me daily–
No Irish shillalah
    Could pommel me so.
Like heart throbs that have me,
Like soul sobs that grieave me,
Whin fearin' ye'll lave me,
    I draam ye say go.

But the silence I broke thus,
Woot the words that I spoke thus,
No adiquate answer raceaived,
    As I talked in this strain of good cheer ;
But I kept up the chat with,
And I spoke this and that with
Bright Bridget, swaat Bridget!
    Oh, Bridget, me dear.

And if I confess them,
(Sure ye'd niver guess them)
So hard to ixpress them,
    The manifold igeas that flowed.
Ye'd think them expinsive,
So vast and extinsive,
So high and intinsive,
    The thributes of illoquence glowed.

Then rest more continted
Woot fwhat I have hinted,
Of the halo that huvered around,
    When footfalls of Bridget fell clear.
But the words I used mainly
Were those I spoke vainly,
Bright Bridget, swaat Bridget!
    Oh, Bridget, me dear.

For me words were not winnin',
I could guess by the grinnin',
Whin from weavin' the linen
    She lifted her eye.
So the luve that had lasted
For years was all wasted.
And whin it had blasted,
    A rint in the sky
Was the visible token,
Of all that luve broken,
And the danger that huvered around
    And ended our courtin' career.
But still I talk nately,
And I dream just as swaatly,
Bright Bridget, swaat Bridget!
    Oh, Bridget, me dear.

TIM O'GRADY.

IF ye'll listen woot contintment
    To an Irish ped'ler's songs—
If ye'll hear wootout resintment
    The tale of all his wrongs—
I'll sing of Tim O'Grady,
    A man of noble birth—
Who ranked woot lord or lady,
    And the dignities of earth.
O'Grady's youth was springlike,
    All flowery, bright and gay,
And future plans were dreamlike,
    And throuble far away.
His fun was all for plisure—
    Fwhativer it might bring—
And if he got full misure,
    His voice tuned up to sing.

O'Grady for a calling
    Quite early went to sea,
But storms were so appalling,
    He thought he wouldn't stay.
So home again at Bogland,
    His father's farm he found,
To cultivate its frogland,
    And dig the turf from ground.

But workin' hard's not aisy,
   Nor diggin' woot a spade,
And though he wasn't lazy,
   He liked to walk down grade.
He thought to be a barber then—
   But he cut a fellow's pate
Amid a wild commotion, when
   He was knocked across the sthreat.
And nixt he thought to run a hearse—
   But the horses took a spree,
And broke the chaise and Paddy's purse
   As bad as they could be.

And thin it was he joined the throops
   To gain a hero's name,
But when he heard the Afghan whoops
   He ceased to think of fame.
He made a sudden, short ratrate,
   Which took him to the rear—
He thought his safety more complate
   Where none but friends were near.
The officers upbraided him
   For running from the field,
And said that it degraded him,
   And that his doom was sealed.
The officers a judgment held,
   And talked it *pro* and *con*,

And said by law they were compelled
　　One course to act upon.
Poor Tim was thin condimned to go,
　　On Friday of that week,
To lands that mortals cannot know,
　　And do not care to seek.
But Tim was very slow to start
　　Wootout his own consint,
And studied, woot a willin' heart,
　　Some process to prevint.
But he beneath the Lion's paw
　　Could find no sure raceipt,
To dodge the dreadful opening jaw,
　　And save his life complete.

So whin the awful Friday came,
　　Woot true Hibernian grace
And glory in a soldier's name,
　　He marched unto the place.
The soldiers fired straight at Tim,
　　And down he groaning fell—
One shot went through the coat of him,
　　And one his hat as well.
But not a bit of flesh was struck,
　　Nor drop of blood was shed—
Tim snatched that piece of sudden luck
　　And palmed himself for dead.

The soldiers turned and went away,
    Delaying funeral rite,
Tim took a squint and then did say,
    "I bid ye boys good-night."
And then, with leap like mountain goat,
    He bounded out of view—
He left ambition there afloat
    And sought for pastures new.

And nixt he thought to pass the bar,
    And illoquence enjoy,
And woot the lawyers squib and spar,
    And give the court employ.
One day he told the judge he lied,
    And then the judge rajined:
"Your language does not coenside
    Woot gintlemen refined;
O'Grady, you must go to jail
    And rest in solitude,
Unless your friends will bring in bail
    And guarantee it good."
The officers escorted Pat
    And put him in the quay,
But he kept thinkin' this and that
    Until the close of day.
And then he laid upon his bed
    And took a gintle dream—

He thought he saw the way ahead
   To cross that throubled stream.
Nixt day he axed to see the court,
   And made a gallant talk—
He told the Judge he was in spourt
   But now would straighter walk.
And thin the smile the Judge did make—
   It dazzled all around,
It glistened like a frosted cake,
   Or taters on the ground.
He said the prisoner was raleased
   From fine and prison cell—
O'Grady's joy was more inkreased
   Then ounly words could tell.
But he had lost his luve for court,
   For Judges and their ways.
So now he thought he'd find his spourt
   Where brighter prospects plase.

And then he choose the field of luve
   To thry fwhat he could win,
And imitate the turtle dove,
   Woot cooin's from wootin'.
Now hear the words that he did mix
   To win a bouncin' bride—
He stirred them in woot little thricks
   And other jokes beside,

Saranely hear the words he said,
  And how he talked them o'er—
I'll vinture that ye niver read
  The likes of them before.

" O Bridget, I have seen the sun
  Peep over India's mountains,
And I have watched the bison run
  Where flow the western fountains.
And I have seen the Polar snow,
  And Iceland woot its wonders—
Beheld Niagara's constant flow,
  And heard its mighty thunders.
I've been where tropic fruit grows lush,
  And tropic birds sing gaily,
Where tropic shells in glory blush
  And tropic flowers bloom daily.
But Bridget, here's the word of truth,
  I'll speak it now complately—
Yourself's the daystar of me youth,
  So listen to me nately.
When you appear the flowers will fade—
  They'll wither by your splindor,
The birds will cease their serenade,
  And look on you in wonder.
The ocean tide will not be fine,
  Nor sweep the beach so greatly,

Niagara Falls may then resign
   Its claims for being stately.
And flowers of spring will dimly shine —
   They'll dwindle by comparing
Their brightest blush woot those of thine—
   The ones that you are wearing.
And honey bees no sweeats can find
   That will surpass your sweeatness,
And friends of art will all combine
   To worship your compleateness.
The vory dogs will niver bark—
   They wouldn't dare to do it,
The world will play a game of hark
   When you go walkin' through it.
And men will say an angel came,
   And wonder how to treat you,
And Bridget, lisp that angel name
   And worship when they meet you."

"Hush, hush!" was Bridget's quick reply,
   "Now, Tim, be vory aisy,
It's not the truth but all a lie—
   I think ye must be crazy.
And if the truth ye iver knew,
   And still know how to prate it,
I'd think that some might seepin' through
   Your blarney irrigate it."

"Trush, trush, now, Bridget," then says Tim,
  "I cannot see the rason
Ye condesind to talk and whim
  In words so out of sason.
I thought to make a talk as neat
  As ony one could wish it,
And stold young Cupid's best receipt
  Prescribin' how to dish it.
I mixed the words and jined them to
  Sweet igeas I invinted,
And practiced them an avenin' through
  And thought them well presinted.
And when a friend came callin' late,
  I thought to analyze them,
By havin' him the words rapate,
  And thin to critacize them.
But all he said was 'Illigent!
  St. Jarves cannot bate thim;
They're good as Cupid iver sent,
  And nothin' can defate thim.'
His words were like a match to tow,
  Me smouldering hopes ignited;
I thought me heart was all aglow,
  I was so mutch excited.
And all the cinders in me heart,
  That former fires had crusted,

So heated now fell quick apart
    Where long they lay and rusted.
But now I see the brightest blaze
    Of incense I can offer,
Is to your radiance but a haze,
    And makes me seem a scoffer.
But Bridget, I adore your name,
    'Tis nourishment to hunger,
My comforter when others blame—
    It makes me heart beat younger.
And when I thirst, as oft I do,
    'Tis sweet as potteen* to me—
It frishens me to think of you,
    And quickly does renew me.
And Bridget, ye are more to me.
    Than forty years of glory,
I'd live woot you on land or sea,
    Or board in pergatory."

"Trush, trush, now, Tim, ye've said enough,"
    Was Bridget's answer quickly,
" Ye'r talk is puny, wretched stuff—
    'Twould make a dummy sickly.
Ye'd betther stop and take on coal,
    And see fwhat nades reparin',

---

* An Irish name for whiskey.

Or blarney wheels may sase to roll,
  Though not a fig I'm carin'."

"Well, well, now Bridget, by the powers!
  It's hopeful talk ye'r makin'.
Your words are fresh as April showers
  When April buds are wakin.'
Ye say me blarney may prosade,
  Provided it's raplinished.
And so I think you kind indade
  To listen till I've finished.
And all your words are sparkling gems,
  More bright than diamonds' glitter;
They'd sarve a queen for diadems,
  And finely would they fit her.
And, Bridget, when your schmiles begin
  (They are so bright and warmin'),
The chicks will lave their roost within,
  Bekase they think it's mornin'.
And birds will come from sunny lands
  Belavin' spring has found us,
And Puck will call his fairy bands
  To gambol all around us.
And Bridget, if ye'll chant a lay
  Our sorrows thin will perish,
Our throubles quickly will decay
  And all our friendship flourish.

For there's more joy in songs ye sing,
    Than all the sparrow's twitting,
They're swaat as all the signs of spring,
    And aquilly as fitting."

"Tim, Tim, ye's got a talkin' spell,
    For talk is cheeap and plinty,
And Bridget knows yourself too well
    To heead one word in twinty.
But, Tim, I know ye're mighty fine,
    And few there are so splinded,
In you the graces all combine,
    Though somewhat strangely blinded.
Ye'er blarney ways are aisy seen—
    Ye needent dig to find them,
And odther thricks that lay between—
    We'll niver stop to mind them.

But, Tim, I like some ways of thine,
    They hint of great pirfection,
And may your countenance iver shine,
    Complate in each direction.
When nature framed you for a man,
    A jewel she invinted,
Ye'd take the sweepstakes for a plan,
    Though thousands were presinted.

And whin Jim Tool does come to call,
    Ave course I'll kindly greet him,
I'll seat him by the garden wall,
    And thin I think I'll treat him—
But, Tim, me heart will beat for you,
    As warm as summer weather,
And I will wish and wait for you
    Till we can live together."

" Is that ye'r voice, me Bridget dear?
    It's music now ye'r making,
'Tis melody me heart to cheer
    And soothes its throb and quaking.
And now I will go home to rest,
    Woot fuel for swaat dreamin'—
I'll sink like sunset in the west,
    Woot glory 'round me gleamin'."

THE GINTLEMAN THAT PAYS THE RINT.

Over-population and other well-known causes have reduced the Irish peasantry to extreme poverty. The food supply is so limited that many of them scarcely know what the taste of meat is. Some of the more enterprising will sometimes buy or beg a little pig from a neighboring farmer, but the animal so procured is not destined to supply the table of its owner with food. It is carefully reared, fattened and sold, and the proceeds used to pay rent. But the typical Irishman, mirthful even in adversity, tries to make light of his privations and playfully calls the pig "The gintleman that pays the rint."

IT'S here that good peraties grow,
   As choice as ony land can show,
And goats are aquil to the bist
That iver climbed the mountain's crist,
And geease that gabble all around
Are just as fine as can be found;
But there's the bist that nature sint—
The gintleman that pays the rint.

Peratie crops are sometimes poor,
The goats give little milk, 'tis sure,
And feathered geease have few to spare,
They have to kape a coat to ware;
The bees that work wootin the hive,
Use half their store to kape alive,
But for his bourd there's little spint—
The gintleman that pays the rint.

The sason may be cold and wet,
Peratie roots may fail to set;
The landlord may his claims inkrase
And levy on the ducks and geoase.
The goats may stray and not raturn,
The turf may smudge and sase to burn;
But there's the chap that yealds contint—
The gintleman that pays the rint.

The landlord kapes a splindid park,
Woot huntin' dogs that howl and bark,
And graceful deer that quickly bound
To where a covert may be found;
But what are dogs and deer and hare,
And all the game that's over thare,
Compared woot one that's neeatly pint—
The gintleman that pays the rint.

The landlord, woot a coach and four,
Drives in a gallop past the doour,
And whin the paple nod and leer
He little thinks a rival near;
A chap that has four trotters too,
And grunts as much as landlords do,
And has a maw of same extint—
The gintleman that pays the rint.

As long as fortune wares a smile,
Good luck will follow all the while,
But when reverse's head is reared,
'Tis found that luck has disappeared;
And pigs and piggish men must die,
But we'll not stop to rason why;
Dasase did come and then he wint—
The gintleman that pays the rint.

THE GINTLEMAN THAT TAKES THE RINT.

ONE day the noble landlord came,
    From hunting hare and other game;
From snaring nature's little pets,
He came to spread some larger nets.
He told his steward to persue
All those whose rent was over-due,
And not rebate a single cint—
The gintleman that takes the rint.

Oh, dark and dreary was the day
When we had all the rint to pay;
The wind blew chillie from the sea,
And we were poor as poor could be.
Our beast was dead, the crop was spoiled,
And we had naught for which we toiled.
But fwhat was that to make ralint
The gintleman that takes the rint?

Our cabin roof was poorly thatched,
And all our clothes were old and patched,
And little Mollie, wan and thin,
Betrayed the marks where want had been.

And we could find no work to do,
For times were hard the country through.
But that was to his averice vint—
The gintleman that takes the rint.

The steward came to make demand,
And take whativer was at hand.
He took poor little Mollie's chair,
But dare not touch her golden hair;
He took her playthings and my plow,
And things I don't remimber now.
But time will come when he'll rapint—
The gintleman that takes the rint.

The landlord drove us from the doour,
And said we should raturn no more;
And now as wanderers we roam—
We have no place to call our home.
The earth doth yield abundant store,
But men still grasp as heretofore,
And one I think is evil bint—
The gintleman that takes the rint.

Oh, it is very strange indeed,
The cruelty of worldly greed!
It has a power all its own
To turn the heart of flesh to stone;

The poor man's grief, the widow's plea,
Are only heard with apathy.
Like Egypt's king, he'll not ralint—
The gintleman that takes the rint.

Such snobbish men who strut the earth,
Claim all the ground is their's by birth;
A splinded title to be sure,
And one as likely to endure
As mouldering heaps in quick decay,
Which sink to dust and blow away.
And one I know whose day is spint—
The gintleman that thieves the rint.

The beast that scratches in the stye
Will be respected by and by,
As much as he, though in the van,
Who crushes down his fellow-man.
E'en now we can begin to see,
How much alike they two may be-
The grunting beast so ill contint,
And gintleman that growls for rint.

MARY MALUE.

FAR out in the counthry where cabbages grow,
Swaat-corn and peraties and beets in a row;
Where pumpkins soon ripen and cucumbers too—
In that Egypt of plinty lives Mary Malue.

'Tis distant from church, from concert and rink,
But of all the wide world 'tis the best place to think;
For the cabbage is quiet and pumpkins in view,
Are afraid of molesting swaat Mary Malue.

The birds that sing sweetest forget their wild trill,
The youngest mosquito finds time to be still;
The frogs are at rest, they music eschew,
And all through respect for swaat Mary Malue.

The bees and the hornets and insects that sting,
Forget their wild warfare and willingly bring

Their tribute of praise, like swaat honey dew,
To fall on the ears of bright Mary Malue.

The chickens and turkeys and geese are so good,
That fwhativer they say, it is well understood,
Are compliments paid, though long over-due,
To the meekness and grace of swaat Mary Malue.

The rabbits, the squirrels and the crickets held court,
And resolved to pravint all radiculous spourt;
But action was nadeless when good manners grew
Like grass in the path of swaat Mary Malue.

The orphan mosquito found there a ratreat,
And poor Katydid took comfort complate;
And desolate souls, of all color and hue,
Laved there in the light of swaat Mary Malue.

But plisure days shorten, how soon we shall see
Our joys take their flight like the leaves of a tree;

It was thus with the frinds whose sad fate
 we review,
Who cintered their hopes in swaat Mary
 Malue.

She wint to the city, sad day for the wrens,
The frogs and mosquitoes, the ducks and the
 hens;
But when she departed, woot long loud adieu,
They croaked a sad chorus for Mary Malue.

RAILROAD MIKE.

RAILROAD Mike has a janius sublime,
   To get into a mix and out again,
And if he is downed it's but a short time
   Till he's up on his faat and about again.

He's sharp as his pick and bright as his spade,
   And no joker iver could flurry him;
No matther what gossip got out on a raid,
   He niver let balderdash worry him.

Whativer the world and some others may say,
   He answers them well if he cares to,
So quick is his wit there is little delay,
   And he says what he thinks if he dares to.

Woot frinds and companions he kultivates pace,
   And he tries to trate thim all dacently,
And walk through the world woot a gintleman's face,
   And that's fwhat he did until racently.

It's whiskey that siperates dearest of frinds,
   And makes thim conduct so conthrarily,
It makes thim say words that no one intinds,
   And thin the bright world looks so drearily.

When passin' down street Mike met an ould
  chum,
  Whose name was just Jimmy McFinnigen,
Who thought that no drink was the aquil of
  rum,
  So he axed him would now he turn in again.

Mick waited a moment and thin he did yeald,
  How could there be mutch hesitation
    there?
All timperance promises soon he rapaled,
  And accepted his frind's invitation there.

So when they went in the room was all warm,
  And fiddles were playing so cheerily:
The chat and the drink could do him no harm,
  And avenin would glide away merrily.

No church was so warm, no place was so gay,
  No odther latch opened so aisily,
To workmen adrift from the toils of the day,
  Who wanted to chat away lazily.

Two drinks were enough to supply thim
    woot voice,
  Though they kept in the bounds of savility;
But soon they began to mutch loudther rajoice,
  And thought thimsilvs highest gintility.

"Oh, Mick is the grandest of mortals I know,
   But he neeads a few digs to adorn him,"
Said Jimmy, who hit him a neeat little blow,
   Though he spoke not a word for to warn him.

Now if ony one thinks that Mick is the chap
   To be silent when some one is flailing him,
All they have to do is to hit him a rap,
   And see fwhat they get for assailing him.

Mick delt Jim a blow on the pint of his nose,
   That made him quite slow to begin again,
And when they exchanged a few dozen of blows,
   It settled the case of McFinnigen.

But frindship once broken is hard to renew,
   So we should all traat it most tinderly,
And nourish the plant woot fwhativer is due,
   Though it thrives for a sason so slinderly.

Right sorry was Mick when he thought of his frind,
   The racently pounded McFinnigen,
Who suffered for mischief he did not intind,
   When in the saloon he turned in again.

But such is the pinalty timper oft pays,
   Their frindship Mick tried to begin again;
He walked down the street upon subsequent days,
   But niver again woot McFinnigen.

PAT'S VIEWS OF A MOTHER-IN-LAW.

IN sasons when the weather's foul;
   It's in the house I'm stoppin';
It's there that Bridget, dearest soul!
   Does all her work and moppin'.
And fun it is to sit and see
   The kitchen fire blazin',
Woot four small childer on your knee,
   The vory mischief raisin';
And odther childer on the floor,
   There's ten, I think, or nearly,
Besides the ones outside the doour
   Makes fifteen counted fairly.
Enough there is to make a din,
   And scare the ghosts from comin',
Enough to cheer the heart wootin,
   Woot whistelin' and drummin'.
But stranger sound than childer make,
   Or turkeys when they gobble,
Is when ould women undertake
   To rigulate a squabble.

Meat wootout gravy, fish wootout slaw,
Makes a dinner complate woot a mother-in-law;

Bell wootout clapper, cat wootout claw,
But the peace of a house is a mother-in-law.

Woot Bridget's timper I could dwell,
   Bekase we're oft continded;
Fwhat signifyes a little spell,
   When all the spite is inded,
For when I see the signs of wrath,
   And Bridget lookin' lowery,
I set about to smooth a path
   Woot words so sweet and flowery,
That smiles come troopin' down her face,
   To hear me chantin' praises,
And parting frowns let in woot grace
   The sunshine of her gazes.
And then we lead a dacent life
   When no one tries to bother,
For we pravint all nadeless strife,
   And honey one another.
But one there is that has a tongue,
   That makes the windees rattle;
It has a sound like dinner gong,
   Or cowboys drivin' cattle.

Though tea may be tasteless, and meats may be raw,
Continted is man woot a mother-in-law;
Catch fish in a cradle, find pins in the straw,
But the summit of luck is a mother-in-law.

LOVE'S ANTICS.

THEY may talk of the thriumphs invinthers achave,
    And the wonderful things that surround us;
Till we pause to consider how much to belave,
    For fear they mislead and confound us.
They may prate of the antics of gas and of steam,
    And the missages lightning delivers;
Of cars on the track and of boats on the stream,
    And bridges that span the wide rivers.
They may brag of machines that run like a top,
    As if worked by the magic of witches;
That hammer, and scroll, and chisel, and chop,
    Or catch up the inthricate stitches.
They may tell of the wather a chemist can freeze,
    Of the stars that astronimers misure,
Of docthors destroyin' the germs of disease,
    Of the manifold sources of plisure:—
But fwhat will compare woot the genius of luve,
    When Cupid has set it in motion?
Now bold as a lion, now meek as a dove,
    Now deep as the caves of the ocean!

Sometimes it will talk, at other times pout,
   Ye cannot tell how to receave it;
And slily sometimes it will nibble about,
   Or run woot the line that ye gave it.
Sometimes it is cautious, at odther times rash,
   And many more times it is neither;
Sometimes it seeks beauty, at other times cash,
   But seldom it settles on either.
Sometimes ye will find it attindin' the school,
   As one of the seekers of knowledge;
But love, in all ages, has acted the fool,
   Though it come from the halls of a college.
Sometimes, at the church it is seated, sedate,
   And ye think it rasimbles a deacon;
But soon it will wink to a rickognized mate,
   And then your whole theory will weaken.
Sometimes in the cars it is mounted to ride,
   And chats woot a vim entertainin';
Sometimes it will brave over tempest and tide,
   Woot niver a word of complainin'.
Sometimes it will meet you when out for a stroll,
   And treat you so warm and so winnin'—
Ye'll liberate sacrets ye kept in control
   Far back as the very beginnin'.

Sometimes it is moody and struck woot the
    rust,
  And quickly ye then will perceave it—
Ye may crack all your jokes, for ye think
    that ye must,
  But blarney's the thing to relave it.
When out for a ride on the traveled highways,
  It's lucky ye are if ye meet it;
But kape a sharp watch on the graveled by-
    ways,—
  It's likely that there ye may greet it.
The hunther scarce knows the haunts of the
    game,
  Or fishermen where there is spourtin';
But who in creation is able to name
  A country where nobody's courtin'?

HOW CAN POET TUNE THE LYRE?

NOVEMBER sky looked darkly down,
    The dreary night was moonless,
The trees were bare, the fields were brown,
    The minstrel's harp was tuneless.
How can a poet tune the lyre
    And set the world to weeping,
When come no thoughts at his desire,
    And all his powers are sleeping?
How can glad music fill the vale
    When southward birds are flying?
How can sweet fragrance long prevail
    When all the flowers are dying?

Cheer up, my friend, and cease to moan,
    Just hear O'Duffey warble
Melodious notes which, left alone,
    Eradicate all trouble.
He has a voice that can make up
    More sounds than ony reaper,
And, put in motion, would wake up
    The very soundest sleeper;
And when his tune begins to range,
    Ye'd wonder where it's going;
It has a course that's just as strange
    As mill ponds overflowing.

It makes a rapid roaring leap
    Beyond the bounds of trouble;
'Twould drown a tempest on the deep,
    Where billows roll and bubble.

So, though the night be dark and cold,
    We still may have enjoyment,
Woot bits of music manifold,
    To give ourselves employment.
And cream will rise above the curd,
    Though darkness hide the dery,
Then deem it not a thing absurd,
    O'Duffey oft was merry.
Late turning toward the western wild,
    His pilgrim spirit yearning,
He might have seemed misfortune's child
    To people slow discerning.
For sorrow surging through his soul
    Had furrowed lines of anguish,
But niver got beyond control,
    Or laid him up to languish.

His clothes were of a rustic kind—
    No fit had been perfected,
And, oh, the fashion none will find—
    At least it's not expected.

And he was blessed with funny freaks,
    And sober ones that matched them;
They blended like mosaic streaks,
    So neat had Nature patched them,
He didn't care for 'possum pie,
    Or hash in all its phases,
Nor bread made out of bran and rye,
    And all those kind of crazes.
But, oh, he loved the pipe and flute,
    The drum, the horn and fiddles,
The sackbut, psaltery, harp and lute,
    And stories, songs and riddles.

And then he loved the merry fife,
    And banjos gently whirring—
They eased the agonies of life
    His heavy spirit stirring.
But when he tried to start sweet notes,
    He could not always find one,
Though, like the boys that chase the goats,
    He sometimes caught the hind one.
He followed notes through thick and thin,
    Like hound the game pursuing;
He scaled the clefs where few have been,
    All bars and bounds eschewing;

But though old Orpheus kept the lead,
   O'Duffey, next unto him,
Exhibiting tremendous speed,
   Was praised by all who knew him.

But how can poet tune the lyre
   And set the world to weeping,
Since now O'Duffey's left the choir,
   And sordid souls are sleeping?

A FAREWELL TO JENNIE.

How many changes Nature brings,
   And how she strives to please us!
But when the wood with music rings,
   She soon turns 'round to tease us.
'Tis thus that song-birds come, and leave,—
   They tarry but a season;
It's not for us to pine or grieve,
   Or doubt the better reason.
The little flowers come peeping through,
   A moment here, to bless us;
They sweetly smile, with small adieu,—
   How gently they impress us!
But autumn winds begin to blow,
   The Frost King is descending;
The little flowers no longer grow,
   Their leaflets are all bending.
They break beneath the pelting storms,
   They fall, like ripened clover,
Naught now remains but withered forms,
   And life, for them, is over.
The morning sun, with radiance bright,
   Brings warmth, and joy, and gladness,
But soon demure, approaching night,
   Restores the gloom and sadness.

Again 'tis dawn, new day begun,
   Fair promises we gather;
But clouds obscure the noonday sun,
   There's mischief in the weather.
'Tis thus our lives, though low or high,
   Have joys and sorrows many;
And now we bid a sad good-bye
   To birds, and flowers, and Jennie.
But winter, too, cannot remain—
   We look for better weather.
We shall not sorrow or complain,
   But smile, in hope, together;
And when we see sweet spring betide,
   And scatter joys for any,—
We'll open doors and windows wide,
   For birds, and flowers, and Jennie!

PIC-NIC DINNER SONG.

TINKLE, tattle, forks that rattle,—
    Sign of coming noon;
Like a banjo in a battle,
    Sounds the silver spoon.
Tinkle, rattle, plates that prattle
    Of the dinner near;
And we know that girls will tattle,
    If you stop to hear.
Tinkle, rattle, bells of cattle
    Hint of coming cream;
Sober, sound, and nothing hattle,
    Like an eagle's scream.
Chinkle, chinkle, bells that sprinkle
    Little drops of sound;
And we know, by tinkle, tinkle,
    Where the sheep are found.
So we know, by jumble, ramble,
    Boys are on the fly —
See the rascals in a scramble
    Over chicken pie!
And we know, by laughs that mingle,
    Girls are gathered near;
All of them are living single,
    As they now appear.

Cupid says they still are under
  Thirty years and ten;
But the little god will blunder,
  Just as mortal men!
Cupid says they all are pretty—
  That no one disputes;
But the little god is witty,
  Full of shams and moots.
Never take the word of Cupid,—
  Test the truth, my friend!
He that follows him is stupid,
  Losing in the end.

This is how Mike Daley grounded,
  Trusting Cupid's oar,—
Bark was tipped and love was drownded,
  Forty leagues from shore;
And his bark, without insurance,
  Drifted down the bay,
But, by dint of brave endurance,
  He survives to-day.
Rattle, rattle, oh, the prattle,
  Shining forks and spoons —
Hear the talk and all the tattle,—
  What a lot of loons!
Such loud prattle would drown battle,—
  Yet we have no wine!
Let us stop this constant rattle,
  And begin to dine.

DUKE JOHN.

Duke John, may your lordship, your grace,
Ever possess a smiling face;
And may your legal education
Win for you great reputation;
May it surpass our expectation.
We think you, like Bacon, judicious and wise,
And may you, like Erskine, in glory arise,
And may you be truthful, affording surprise.
For miracles are so uncommon,
And the mind of man, poor human,
Is so dull of comprehension.
But failing of such honor, we pray
You'll be sent embassador to Botany Bay.*

* A place to which Great Britain transports criminals.

IRENE.

CUPID, searching for a queen,
    Caught a glimpse of fair Irene.
Rustle of the growing wheat,
Ripple of the waters fleet,
Gleam of gold, or silver spar,
Twinkles of the evening star,—
Could not lure him, for, I ween,
He was blinded by Irene.
Mellow tints or rainbow hues,
Sparkle bright of morning dews,
Tinkle of the bells of sheep,
Winds that waft the daisy's sleep,
Quiet lakes, with silver sheen,—
Could not tempt him from Irene.
Hum of bees 'mid orchard boughs,
Where the little birdlings house;
Ocean shells, and songs, and flowers,
All have lost their magic powers.
Cupid fairer sight has seen—
All his thoughts are of Irene!

DEATH OF AN OLD BACHELOR.

O'ER the pathway of life an old bachelor seared
Took a sorrowful look and then disappeared.
His exit was sudden—poor desolate soul—
He darted from life like a squirrel to his hole.
Yet the movement was quiet, like a star of the sky,
He flickered from sight with no word of good-bye.
The country was roused and inquiry was made,
No one had made note that so soon he would fade.
No one could explain it, all theories combine,
Revealed not the cause of his sudden decline;
But people were restless and wanted to know
The cause of this sudden, o'er-shadowing woe.
The coroner came and examined each bone,
But declared that the cause of his death was unknown.
The doctors then came and a council was held,
To see if such mystery might be dispelled,

They looked at the face, but it seemed as serene
As the moon at its full when no clouds intervene;
They bent o'er the form, they got down on their knees,
But they saw not the symptoms of any disease.
So, filled with a purpose to save other lives,
They drew out their lancets and ground up their knives.
They examined the brain, but they found no defect,
It was better by far than they could expect;
And the lungs were as sound as a crab-apple green,
Not a pimple upon them was there to be seen.
The throat was as perfect as any could wish,
Capacious and wide as the gill of a fish;
But picture you may, how the doctors all start,
When probing still deeper they come to the heart.
As fishers long toiling pull net to the shore,
And capture the game that was wily before,

They tugged at his heart, but they found it as big,
As a cistern that's empty and quite out of rig.
They thumped and they thumped but it only said "Thug,"
In a tone that resembled an old empty jug.
And worse and still worse, more misfortune befell,
When they found that his heart was beginning to swell.
They wonderingly watched till it grew so immense,
It filled up the yard and then broke down the fence.
A dog that stood by was so scared by the crash,
That he made a short turn and ran home with a dash.
The doctors were frightened and hid in a tree,
And waited to see what the issue would be.
The process continued; it grew all the while,
Till it covered the country for over a mile.
And then, as all danger will sometime be o'er,
It settled itself and expanded no more.

The doctors, now thinking it safe to draw near,
Dismissed all their doubts and came down with a cheer.
But how to explore this huge mountain of flesh,
Examine each gulf and unravel each mesh,
Was a task that appalled them; they feared to explore
A country where no one had traveled before.
So acting with caution they went to a hill,
And climbed to the top of a flouring-mill.
With spy-glasses furnished they gazed at the sight,
But they saw not a thing that afforded delight.
Like the marks on the moon all disfigured it lay,
With ledges of rock that seemed ashen and gray;
And gorges and caves that no doubt were so deep,
Some demon had dug them and gone down to sleep.
And river beds dry and all sprinkled with bones,
And shells that had washed from the fartherest zones;

And trunks of old trees, and billows of sand,
That tempests of ages had garnered and fanned.
And rocks that were scattered as if giants at play,
Had tossed them about on some grand holiday.
The doctors concluding to closer approach,
Now sent to the city and ordered a coach.
They drove to the top of the heart with all speed,
But found it a desolate country indeed;
Not a blade of green grass, not a twig or a flower,
Not the sign of a bud to beguile a sad hour,
Not a form to caress, not a thing to delight—
'Twas the home of old Chaos and haunt of the night.
But relics they found which made it appear,
That in ages gone by it was tenanted there;
Some wish-bones of chickens, now hardened to stone,
And walls of a mansion with moss overgrown,
And on it inscribed these words were still seen:
"I lived upon promise with blarney between,

But a drouth coming on, when nothing would grow,
I packed up my things, and have moved down below.
Just turn to the right till you come to a mound,
On the north is a door at which you must pound.
If no one makes answer, then pound quite severe,
For down in this country 'tis hard to make hear.
But ere you come in, bid your friends all adieu,—
'Tis the last they will look upon any of you;
For down in this region of flower and fern,
So delighted all comers, they never return;
And so balmy the air, and so healthy the shore,
That they who dwell here will live evermore!"
The doctors, excited, with footsteps quite fleet,
Proceeded to follow directions complete.
They came to the mound, and on entering there,
They gazed on a world most surprisingly fair.

There were groves of red roses, and hedges of flowers;
There was highlight and twilight, and sunshine, and showers;
There were mountains and valleys, and rivers that wind
Through orchards and meadows, with woodlands behind;
There were birds of bright plumage, and bees on the wing;
There were lilies, and lilacs, and splendors of spring,
It was Eden itself in miniature form,—
Except that, at times, it was somewhat too warm.
The doctors, delighted, determined to stay,
So they asked for a lot how much they must pay.
Four hundred and fifty a foot, they were told,
And payment must be in the purest of gold;
For business was brisk, and the place on a boom,
And all the hotels were crowded for room.
But soon they found shelter, no one need depart,—
There's a welcome for all in a bachelor's heart!

And now the world knows the cause of his death:
It was not on account of a shortness of breath;
It was not disappointment—a thousand times no!
That brought on the world this horrible woe.
His heart, overloaded, broke down with the weight,—
And that was, as usual, the bachelor's fate!

FOUR FAIR MAIDS.

WINTER, Summer, Autumn, Spring,
    Then's the time for everything.
Spring is when we plant tomatoes,
Autumn's when we dig potatoes,
Summer's when Spring birds are older,
Winter's when the days are colder.
Winter, Summer, Autumn, Spring,
Then's the time for everything.

Spring is when fair maidens, looming,
Beat the roses in their blooming;
Summer's sweets and they, combining,
Pale the stars in glory shining.
Autumn's frost, I pray you linger,—
Glove awhile your icy finger.
Winter, wait, and be forbearing—
Four fair maids are young and daring.

Wait till they, so sweet and tender,
Find a strong and true defender!
Wait till they, so young and growing,
Learn that thimbles are for sewing!
Wait till they will bravely risk it,—
That they know light bread from biscuit;
Then, if favoring winds are blowing,
Proper time has come for going!

Winter, Summer, Autumn, Spring,
Then's the time for anything.
Catch the trout, or track the beaver,—
Find your love, and never leave her;
Plant the pansy, pluck the daisy,—
Why should we be slow or lazy?
Gladden life with harmless pleasure,—
Let us have our dues' full measure,
In Winter, Summer, Spring or Fall,—
We want them then, or not at all!

A VALENTINE.

You are my darling,
 I am your beau;
You are a jewel,
 Undoubtedly so.

I am a lover,
 Living in doubt;
You are a mystery
 Past finding out.

I am but common,
 While you are *bon ton;*
My home is a cottage,
 And yours a *salon.*

I eat when at dinner,
 You pick at dessert;
I come to court you,
 And you act the flirt.

My garb is the russet,
 In silk you attire;
I journey on foot,
 And you ride with the squire.

A VALENTINE.

I am no singer,
   Your voice is a bird's;
Ye seraphs keep silent!
   Or hum her sweet words.

And you are a jewel,
   A brilliant, a gem;
A rose of October,
   The last on the stem.

A fairy, an angel,
   The brightest one, too;
Accept this short ditty,
   Then, darling, adieu.

A HORSE IS A HORSE.

A HORSE is a horse, and a mule is a mule,
  No matter how much you may speed them;
A man is a man, and a fool is a fool,
  No matter what food you may feed them.
A dog is a dog, whatever his bark,
  No matter how well you may treat him;
A hog is a hog, though kept in a park,
  Or anywhere else that you meet him.
A man may inhabit a house that is fine,
  Surrounded by all that is fairest,—
May feast upon honey, and mutton and wine,
  And dainties, the best and the rarest;
His galvanized manners may make him appear
  Superior to servants about him,—
May fill a poor yeoman with awe and with fear,
  Till he dares to do nothing without him;
But who would be jealous of such a man's state,
  For the little short day that he thrives in?
For the pigmy aims and the petty hate,
  And the shriveled-up heart that he hives in? —

For wealth cannot make a gentleman fine,
    When habit a beast has enrolled him—
It's only the casting of jewels to swine,
    To honor or try to uphold him.
But he is a man whose heart is still warm,
    No matter how fortune may frown him;
Who labors for good, and never for harm,
    And, by-and-by, angels will crown him!

WELCOME TO SPRING.

SPRING with her smiling face
   Welcome we here!
Where was her hiding place
   All the long year?
Down in the vale below,
Down where the lilies grow—
Nook that the seasons know,
   Where none can peer.

Spring has a step so light—
   No one can hear;
But when the sky grows bright,
   Then she is near.
Winds hint of her advance,
Fountains begin to dance,
Birds know there's no mischance—
   Yes, she is here.

Spring will not long abide,
   Soon she will go;
Down where the seasons hide,
   Far down below.
Soon will her flowerets fold,
Beauty be turned to mould,
Sadly her story told—
   Queen of the year.

Maiden with forehead fair,
   Face with a smile;
Silken and shining hair,
   Wait for a while.
Keep the sad hours at bay,
Drive the dark clouds away,
Liven the dullest day—
   Maiden so young.

Maiden with eyes of brown,
   Welcome we you;
On thee no shadows frown,
   All the year through.
May peace with thee abide,
Pleasure with thee reside,
And naught of ill betide,
   All the year long.

Maiden, you too must go
   Time may be near;
When, in the vale below,
   Daisies will hear.
Winds of the Autumn moan,
Here rests the fair alone,
And now her name's unknown—
   Maiden so rare!

Maiden, they are not true—
  Such words so sad;
We shall remember you,
  And shall be glad.
Earth may engulf thy form,
Tempests around thee storm,
Naught can dispel thy charm—
  Maiden so fair!

"SMOKER JIM."

PRELUDE.

FOREVER honored be Queen Bess,
   Great Britain's maiden queen!
Thanks to her royal mightiness,
  Tobacco first was seen,
    Within the realm of England.
Sir Walter brought it from the West,
From out the land that we love best.
Oh, sweetly may his spirit rest,—
  Raleigh, of England!

SONG.

Oh, the pleasures of the smoker,
  As he puffs his pipe!
Isn't he a jolly joker
  Of that noble type,
Who never rouse a settled sorrow,
Put off weeping till the morrow,
Loan their cares, but do not borrow?
  Bless the pipe!

Oh, the glory of the smoker,
  As he whiffs his cigar!
Isn't he a happy joker,
  With a wit that leaves no scar?

How he smiles with all his features,
How he loves his fellow-creatures,—
Puffs, in praise of worthy teachers,
   The cigar!

Oh, the peace that soothes the smoker,
   As he draws his cigar!
He that hates him is a croaker,
   Carrying blame too far.
How he lifts his feet and poses,
How he nods and how he dozes,
As in sleep his vision closes,—
   Blessed cigar!

Ever honored be the smoker
   As he puffs with cheer;
Better far to be a toper
   Of tobacco than of beer!
See the smoke about him hover,
Faithful as an ardent lover,—
What a light and fairy cover,—
   Smoke so clear!

Now, I know a witty smoker,—
   Some have called him "Jim,"—
For he is a jolly joker,
   And can sing a hymn.

How his voice will pitch and roll
From the caverns of his soul,
Till it reach some distant goal
   Known to him!

And this jolly, pleasant smoker,
   Happy angel, Jim!
Soars above the common croaker,
   Like the seraphim.
And though sorrow may subdue him
Still we trust it can't get to him,
Far above it now we view him—
   Noble Jim!

But this worthy social smoker
   Sprightly, merry Jim;
Shrewd and comic as a joker,
   You may picture him.
Pays his debts if so he please,
Creditors can cough and wheeze,
When he settles they may sneeze—
   Spendthrift Jim!

But, again, this worthy smoker,
   Truly social Jim,
Never paints his face with ochre,—
   All should honor him.

For his acts are not deceiving,
All he says is worth believing,
Worlds would weep to see him grieving—
 Friendly Jim!

Blessings on the jolly smoker,
 Happy, witty Jim!
With a common broom and poker,
 Keep your mustache trim.
And may winter winds pass by thee,
Prowling dangers fail to spy thee,
Tropic heat can never dry thee—
 Humid Jim!

But 'tis feared this social smoker
 Kind and friendly Jim,
May be fleeced by some vile broker,
 Or by lawyers grim.
Smoking will not sate his hunger,
Smoking will not make him stronger,
Credit he can get no longer—
 Needy, luckless Jim!

Who will keep the poor old smoker?
 Slouchy, sloven Jim!
He that was a jolly joker,
 Can but scold and whim.

Wintry age has found him needy,
With old clothes all torn and seedy,
Curses on a habit greedy—
  Such as followed Jim.

A BOY'S WISHES.

CHILDREN'S years are very long,
   Nights and days move slow.
Wish that I was big and strong,
   Then I'd dare to go
Up the street and on the hills—
   I'd drive the horses, too;
I'd make the engines run the mills,
   And push the work right through!

I'd show the world what I could do,—
   I'd wander far and wide;
I'd travel every country through;
   I wouldn't walk—I'd ride.
I wouldn't be afraid to go,
   Because I'd have a gun;
And all the robber Indians know
   That I would never run!

The school-room is a dreary place;
   They keep us all day through—
I'd rather go and run a race,
   Or stay out here with you.
I'm 'fraid the time will never come
   When I will be a man,—
When I can go and leave my home,
   And follow out my plan.

I wish that I could thrash Tom Brown—
   He thinks he's mighty big!
He knocked my little brother down,
   And broke my whirligig.
And I would like to skate as fast
   As Billy Jones, and Fred;
I wouldn't let them get apast,—
   I'd keep ten feet ahead!

Last night we boys had lots of fun,
   It's fun to catch a fish,
I caught thirteen, and Billy none—
   He didn't get his wish.

But Billy is the greatest chap,
   That ever wore a shoe;
One day he snatched Will Jenkins' cap,
   And tore it right in two.
But when the teacher found it out,
   He sent out Jimmy Vance
To cut a little hickory sprout—
   And didn't Billy dance?

I wish that it was winter time,
   And I could run and slide;
I like to hear the sleigh-bells chime,
   And see the fun beside.

And winter's when the Christmas comes,
    For you and me and all;
Some boys get sleds and others drums—
    I want a rubber ball.

These summer days are dreadful long,
    When will they all go by?
We boys are getting old and strong,
    And most ashamed to cry.
The little chaps we don't molest,
    We let them have their play,
We older boys will work our best,
    But I must say good day.

A MOTHER'S CARE.

AS birds from Northern lands take flight,
   When falling leaves give warning;
As travelers, on approach of night,
   Make halt and wait for morning;
As sailors, on the surging seas,
   Look, anxious, for the harbor;
As lonesome woodmen leave the trees,
   When night is darkening over;
As soldiers, in the tented field,
   Look homeward with deep yearning
As wanderers, on the distant wild,
   Think fondly of returning;
As miners 'merge from damp and gloom,
   To bask in sunlight's greeting;
As city folks in fields find room
   For freer, happier meeting：—
So, to the child, the mother's heart
   Is comfort, shelter, cover;
When grief would rend his soul apart,
   She spreads a healing over.
The falling tears are scarce begun,
   When kindly words are proffered—
"Don't cry," and "Never mind, my son,"
   And soft hands stroke his forehead.

The child is calmed, his sorrows cease,
    His heart beats brave, and stronger;
The troubles that disturbed his peace
    Are vexing him no longer.
The little man mature has grown,
    The marks of years are on him;
But never shall he cease to own
    The love bestowed upon him.
And never can the debt be paid,
    Maternal care imposes.
Like lilies in the field arrayed,
    Like distant blooming roses,—
Far out of reach and in the past,
    On memory's upland growing,
Kind actions live whose blooms will last,
    Whose fragrance, ever blowing,
Make glad the heart and warm the life
    With kindlier, better feeling
Than in the wicked whirl of strife,
    Where selfishness, prevailing,
So often fills the heart with gall,
    And makes men hate each other.

JUNE.

COME, merry, gay month, come, June, with your roses,
   We welcome you here as our guest,
With all the wild flowers that summer discloses,
   O make this your home and here rest!

In seasons before you seemed but a caller,
   Just bowing a greeting, then gone—
Were those your best visits, and shall they grow smaller,
   As time with his cycles rolls on?

O merry June month, you came tripping so lightly,
   With squirrels, with birds and with bees;
We trust you will treat these young friends all politely,
   And make them here feel at their ease.

Ill bred it would be now to leave us abruptly,
   Dispersing this gay, happy throng;
And they shall be punished who act thus corruptly,
   Inflicting so senseless a wrong.

We'll try, merry month, to be more entertaining,
  We, and this circle of friends!
We hope that no one will have cause for complaining,
  Before this glad gathering ends.

O what shall be theme for pleasant conversing,
  Of what shall we talk for a while?
Of love or of war, or old stories rehearsing—
  Or how shall we summon a smile?

The meadow-lark chirps and the robin is calling,
  They seem to be happy and gay;
The brook bass frisks riot where bright waters falling,
  Run frothing and foaming away.

The herds move apace to green pastures inviting,
  They sport like a boy at his play—
Oh, sure it is sweet if it is not exciting,
  When summer unfolds such a day.

The little lad, tired of study, is wishing
    For orders to lay up his books;
It would be such an excellent day to go fishing,
    Or bathe in the babbling brooks.

And soon as released right out he goes bounding,
    He has not a moment to lose;
He jumps and he shouts, and the echoes resounding,
    Proclaim the wild path he pursues.

O face of the child, thou art part of our summer,
    Thy laugh and thy smiles are a share;
We welcome thee here, thou little newcomer,
    So free from the burden of care.

You mingle your shouts with the songs of the thrushes,
    You sing in this chorus of glee;
You gambol as gay as the river that rushes
    Its waters far down to the sea.

And over the meadows the sunshine is sleeping,
    The mist on the hills moveth slow;
While loitering kine come leisurely creeping
    From out of the valley below.

And down in the valley the lilies are waiting,
  All decked in a clothing of bloom;
They care not for praise or for fame's highest
      rating—
  They wait to make bright the sick room.

The lilies are kind and never contending,
  They live as a lesson for men.
Their beauty is sweet, as humility bending—
  We bless them again and again.

O merry June month, so rich are your
      treasures—
  You come as a queen in her state;
You scatter around us the rarest of pleasures,
  Your mission is love and not hate.

Your bounty is great, but the wealth of your
      coffers
  Supports the high rank that you hold;
You temper the chill of the world and its
      scoffers,
  Wherever your sunbeams have strolled.

You came, merry month, in the seasons'
      procession,
  But let them their journey pursue;
Abide thou with us till we make full confession
  Of the love that we cherish for you.

FEARS AND TEARS.

As mountain deer will sometimes bound
   At the fancied bark of a huntsman's hound,
So a child asleep on its mother's arm
Will sometimes leap from dream of harm;
His piteous cry reveals his fears,
And he pours them forth in floods of tears.
But the little face, so wild and wet,
Will not disbar a mother's pet
From kisses that kill the ghouls of fright,
Or drive them back in the realms of night.
And sleep reclaims the little form,
As shepherd shelters from the storm.
But evil days pursue the child,
He fears the dark and dreads the wild;
He looked for a stronger hand to lead,
And thought the world was wide indeed—
He tripped and fell and cried in pain,
But sprang on his feet and was off again;
And the child went on with the years that ran,
And the boy gave place to the full grown man.
But where are the tears of his childhood's face?
Can we find a hint of their hiding-place?

They have left no trace that we can see,
In the buried past they all must be.
But the heart of the man doth sometimes still
Have a touch as keen as winter's chill;
And meaning more than childhood's cry,
He draws his breath with a heavy sigh—
But the pride of the man doth hold control,
And he checks the storm in his troubled soul.
Yet times there are when sorrow deep
Unmans the heart and warriors weep.
O, who hath strength to conquer grief?
Destroy its power or make it brief?
Do we not hear the wide world's moan?
Do we not heed the undertone
Amid the lulls of the warring world,
When strife asks truce and flags are furled;
A saddened sound like the sobbing sea,
Which hints of wrecks that afar may be;
A murmur like the winds that wave
The treetops round a lonely grave;
And like the winds that plough the main,
And like the storms that bow the grain.
So sorrow ranges far and near,
And takes the tribute of a tear
From man and child, from rich and poor,
And dogs their steps from door to door,

Then days grow dark and nights are cold,
And men of strength grow weak and old;
And frost works death and flowers decay,
And birds of spring are flown away.
Yet, wintry gloom, you too must go!
The warming sun will melt the snow;
And grass will green the hill and slope,
And spring will sow the seeds of hope.
The somber skies will light to blue,
And let the birds come flocking through.
And boats will sail along the shore,
And flowers will bloom as heretofore;
And time will come when war will cease,
When men will live in perfect peace;
When ripened fruit of good seed sown
Will bless mankind in every zone.

DAY-BREAK.

IF winter reigns haughtily all through the hills,
   And there's snow in the valleys below;
If ice has fettered the flowing rills,
   And the flowers no longer grow;
If chilling winds from the cold Northeast
   Have driven the birds away;
If flocks no longer can find a feast
   In the fields, though they search all day;
If leaden skies shed somber light,
   And land and sea seem drear—
Shall we say that the world is doomed to night
   And darkness all the year?
Shall we look no more for opening spring,
   And the violet's purple bed?
Shall we hear no more the rustling wing
   Of the wild bird overhead?
Shall spring and summer cease to be,
   And their works of love resign,—
No leaves to cover the maple tree,
   No flowers to flush the vine?

But spring *will* come; the balmy days,
   Though seeming distant still,
Are marching, on appointed ways,
   Their mission to fulfill.
No power of earth can hinder now
   The march of the coming spring;
The birds will sing in the greenwood bough,
   While the woods with music ring.

And better days for men will dawn,
   Than we are passing through.
The powers of truth are pressing on,
   And making all things new.
For I know that the world is tired of strife,
   Of the dizzy din of war;
And I know that it longs for a better life
   Than in years that have gone before.
I know that it hates the hateful man,
   And the arts that makes deceit;
I know what it thinks of fields where ran
   Red blood on the trampled wheat.

I know that it loves the kind and good,
   And the generous, loving heart;
And words of praise, when understood,
   Are for those who have a part

In raising up to a higher plane
    The struggling and oppressed,
Who, toiling onward, try to gain
    Their rights, and peace, and rest.

But around us lies a stricken camp,
    Annoyed by pains and fears;
The victims of the cold and damp,
    And the sins of six thousand years.
The malice, the pride and hateful lust,
    That, all through the centuries past,
Have turned the flower of man to dust,—
    Shall their ravages always last?
Shall sin and sorrow never cease,
    Nor battle's deadly shock?
And when the angels sang of peace,
    Did they only mean to mock?

As God is God, as the seasons come
    We look for a better spring,
When earth shall be a peaceful home,—
    When joy in everything
Shall prove the love of the power that holds
    The helm of the moving spheres,—
Of Him who in his wisdom molds
    The events of all the years.

But what are the signs of morning break,—
  Or are we far in the day?
Is the watchman on Mt. Sear awake
  To the brightness of its ray?
As clouds may oft obscure the light,
  When the orb of day has risen—
We may be farther from the night,
  And nearer out of prison
Than wise men think, who, in the schools
  Of grave experience, make a chart
And think, by the use of common rules,
  To measure the great world's heart!

Some have no hope, and think a change
  For future good is not in store,—
The door, still swinging on its hinge,
  Will swing, they say, no farther than before.
They little think what the Ruling Power
  May bring to pass in a day;
They little know what flying hour
  May bring new laws into play!
They little think of the love of God,
  And the word of the Sacred Book,—
That the plowshare shall supplant the sword,
  The spear yield to the pruning-hook.

And when the Savior spake to some,
   And a form of prayer had given,
He bade them say, "Thy kingdom come,"
   And "Thy will on earth as in heaven."
And in the prayer the Savior used,
   Did the words no meaning make?
Or is our language now abused
   When we say, "For Jesus' sake"?

We cannot see as from Patmos Isle,
   The scroll of Time unrolled,
But we can note events meanwhile,
   And know what the past hath told.
So, back in the past we search to see,
   How much of good is lost;
If men were better, the world more free,
   In ages that are past.
And if the night grows still more dark,
   If the lights within burn low;
If right and truth are but a spark,
   Or but an after-glow;
If the Savior's life was of little note,
   And the martyrs died in vain,
If all the good who ever wrote,
   Have failed to make truth plain;

If wrong is stronger than the right,
   And the powers of ill increase,
Let us leave the field and no longer fight,
   But sue for terms of peace.
But if the world has made advance,
   From history's earliest dawn,
Who will not say there is a chance—
   The work may still go on.

A SCHOOL-GIRL'S GREETING TO AUTUMN FLOWERS.

AUTUMN flowers, what has delayed you
    That you came so late?
Were all the garments Nature made you
    Old and out of date?
Did you stop to trim and fit them,
    Fashion them with care?
Did you wait to slowly knit them
    Into shapes they are?
Was it hard to make selections
    When you came to choose
Colors for your fair complexions
    From all rainbow hues?
Did the shop boy come as ordered
    With your package new?
Were your 'kerchiefs neatly bordered,
    Such as suited you?
Milliners are *so* provoking,
    How they fuss and mix;
They have learned the art of poking
    Patience out of fix.
Did the druggist send the powder
    That you wanted soon?
Did he mix it worse than chowder,
    Like a silly loon?

A SCHOOL-GIRL'S GREETING TO FLOWERS.

Tell me now what did delay you?
    Vex me not, I pray!
And I'm sure I'll not betray you—
    What have you to say?
Did a drunken coachman blunder
    Driving out of course;
And, if so, may I not wonder,
    You have fared no worse?
O, you flowers are slow replying,
    And I can not wait—
There's no reason for denying,
    I know why you're late.
I saw you straying in the hollows,
    When I came from school;
You were playing with the swallows,
    Close beside the pool.
Some of you were in the hedges,
    Hiding, so I think;
Some were seated in the sedges,
    Watching ducklings drink.
In the woodlands some were tripping,
    To the music of the trees;
In the brooklet some were dipping,
    Sipping at their ease.
Some away on distant meadows,
    Thinking no one near,
Were flirting with the passing shadows,
    Making signs so queer!

To the shadows they were nodding,
　　To the shadows shy,
But the shadows onward plodding,
　　Only said good-bye.
Now you hiding in the rushes,
　　Do not wish to hear,
But I see your modest blushes,
　　And will give you cheer.
I forgive you for delaying,
　　All the summer long;
Since you are no longer straying,
　　I forgive the wrong.
I forgive you for your beauty,
　　Such my love for you—
It is but a pleasant duty,
　　Friendship to renew.
The birds have gone—they did forsake me—
　　Their friendship was not strong;
They did not offer once to take me,
　　To where the summer's long.
The bees have settled in their dwelling,
　　And closed their doors to me;
When they come out there is no telling
　　Where you and I shall be.
The miser squirrels have gathered riches
　　Like castled knights they dwell,
Sequestered in secluded niches,
　　They hold their plunder well.

And so mere summer friends will vanish,
  They will not long remain—
What little bars avail to banish
  The insincere and vain!
But lingering flowers, I will caress you,
  On winter's marge so drear,
You come to me and now I bless you,
  That you are gathered here.
You come when other friends are leaving,
  You are so good and kind!
You come to comfort me when grieving,
  And make me more resigned.
Oh, tarry with me long, I pray you,
  And cheer me on my way;
Though I cannot now repay you,
  For the pleasure of to-day.
I know that wintry winds will numb you,
  When your leaves are rolled;
Frost will seem to overcome you,
  So exposed to cold.
Your wraps are light for winter weather,
  But, though you grow chill,
Spring will find you all together—
  Life remaining still.
Spring will strew the earth with roses,
  For the wise and true;
Every turn in life discloses
  Beauty, still in view.

Every land is strewn with flowers,
   E'en cold Labrador;
Wide the circuit of their powers,
   Blessing every shore.
Deep old ocean cannot drown them!
   There they dwell secure;
Death itself but seems to crown them
   Brighter than before.
So I think their race immortal,
   On the other shore.
Just beyond the shining portal,
   Flowers bloom forever more.
Only now I cannot name them,
   Roses, lilies they may be;
But I have the faith to claim them
   For a land I do not see.
Flowers of earth! you do assure me,
   Of a better life;
And your gentle ways allure me
   From the paths of strife.
Here I know I shall have losses—
   Things to vex and to annoy;
But I'll count them trifling crosses
   When I reach the land of joy.
Here our best laid plans are thwarted,
   Things we value disappear;
And the world oft seems distorted—
   Running out of gear.

A SCHOOL-GIRL'S GREETING TO FLOWERS. 111

Dante fain would paint so brightly *
   For Beatrice; but the spell
Broken was by scenes unsightly
   And intrusions that befell,
Ere the picture was completed:
   From the city callers came;
Dante's project they defeated,—
   Robbing art of his high name.
From the story so impressing,
   Fancy can supply
But a poor, imperfect guessing
   Of a work that should not die.
Oh, the pictures not completed!
   Oh, the plans that yield to fate!
But we'll not give up, defeated,—
   Flowers and victory oft are late.

---

* Dante once sat down to paint a picture of an angel, for Beatrice. He was interrupted by callers from the city, and, laying aside the work, never finished it.

THE SNOW STORM.

Of all the storms that sail the air,
   Or sweep the earth below,
There is none half so fair—
There is none to compare—
   With white-flaked winter snow.

The winds that fitful round us stray,
   We know not where they go;
Sometimes they play,
Sometimes they slay—
   We trust them not as snow.

The mists that hang about the steep
   May hover where they grow;
Like babes they creep,
Or sometimes sleep—
   They do not frisk as snow.

The fogs have followed a strange pursuit;—
   They are worse than winds that blow;
They boldly dispute
The brave mariner's route—
   They are more to dread than snow.

The rain so often makes a call,
  Its footsteps well we know;
It blesses rich and poor and all—
We love to hear it gently fall,
  Though not so gay as snow.

The hail is rough, uncouth and plain,
  It loves to pelt and throw;
It beats down the grain,
The young lambs are slain—
  It's more severe than snow.

The sleet is sister to the hail,
  And plays a patter low;
It sallies out in any gale,
And cares not whom it may assail—
  It's not so mild as snow.

So, of all the storms that sail the air
  Or sweep the earth below,
There is none half so fair—
There is none to compare
  With the fairy, feathery snow.

And thus it is that falling light,
  As it whitens earth below,
It hints of a land forever bright,
Of a country where there is no night,
  And all is pure as snow.

WHY SHOULD AUTUMN BID ADIEU?

WHY should Autumn bid adieu,
   And take our golden treasures?
Has it no calling to pursue
   But rob us of our pleasures?
The little flowers that summer left,
   What harm to let them linger?
It seems an act of petty theft
   When Autumn's frosty finger
Coils round our little blooming friends,
   And shrivels forms so tender.
O Autumn, you make small amends
   For such a gross offender!
And then the songs of birds you take,
   On winds that howl and drivel;
You find not one excuse to make
   For activity so uncivil.
And Autumn, you deceived us so,
   We loved when first we met you
In purple, gold and garnet glow,
   All Nature seemed to pet you.
To you was given mellow fruit
   And ripened nuts well crowned you,
And Indian summer for your suit
   Hung gently all around you.

And golden corn was in your keep,
  And golden-rod and heather,
And on green hill, the grazing sheep,
  Strayed on in mellow weather.
And working bees plied at their task—
  They sipped your blooming clover;
And every thing that you could ask
  Or wish was given over.
No other season boasts such wealth
  As to you has succeeded,
And yet you take from us, by stealth,
  What we would give if needed.
Now why should you bid us adieu,
  And take our golden treasures?
Have you no calling to pursue,
  But rob us of our pleasures?
Oh yours is like the greed of man!
  No riches ever sent him
Prevent him grasping all he can,
  Or very well content him.

www.ingramcontent.com/pod-product-compliance
Lightning Source LLC
Chambersburg PA
CBHW030404170426
43202CB00010B/1490